...he Hero left... no safe...

slowly recovering in the warm Dark...

The seed slumbers within...

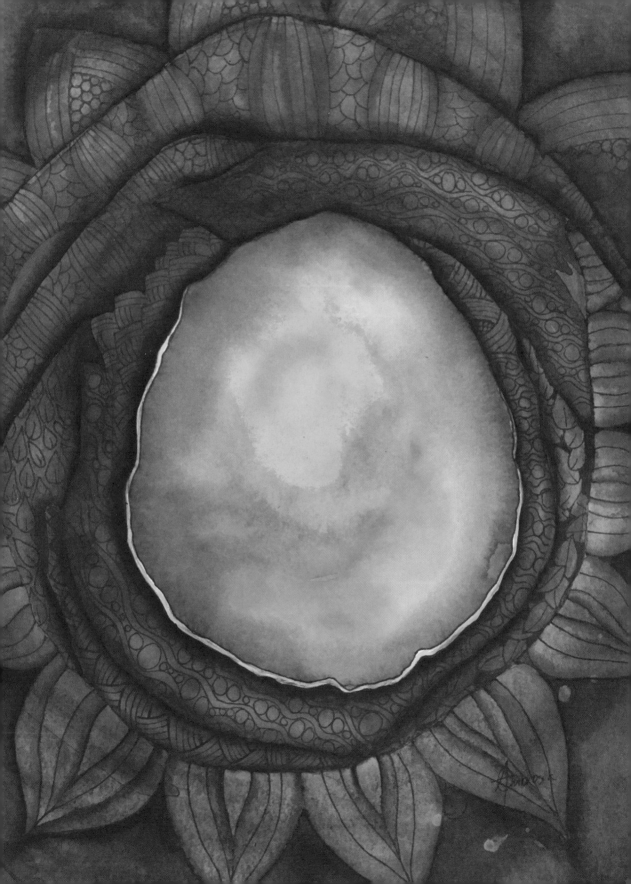

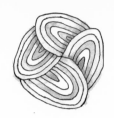

Contents

CHAPTER ONE

To the broken-hearted

So many things can break our hearts.

Relationships break up. Long-term friendships explode and dissolve. Death can take a friend, a parent, a partner, or a child. And, the loss breaks something in us.

A vital part of ourselves dies when we lose someone we love. Our hearts crack open, revealing a gaping emptiness where there used to be feelings of love, safety and connection.

Our heart is one of the hardest things to heal because we don't talk about it.

Our busy lives don't leave us space to grieve, to express the pain we feel nor reconcile the loneliness. Yet, so many of us stagger on, carrying the vast weight of our grief with us, unexpressed and unhealed.

In older, kinder times, people were graced with a year of mourning after losing a loved one. Wearing black was a signal to those around you that you were in a dark state and could not be expected to behave or cope as you normally would. This gave the grieving person space to be miserable in peace and quiet.

Many saner cultures have rituals that allow for the expression of grief, such as paid wailers at funerals, the rending of clothes, or the ritual cutting of hair or the skin. There are funeral rites that go on for months instead of the puny one-off things we do in Western society. In all cultures, just as in ours, after the appropriate time of mourning is deemed over, we are expected to go back to our normal lives. And, it doesn't work.

Statistics show that many married couples die within a year of each other. As a nurse, most of the suicide attempts I saw in emergency and psychiatric wards were due to relationship breakups. People truly do die of a broken heart!

An older man was brought into emergency by ambulance one day. His wife had died in her sleep, and when he woke and found her, he had a heart attack. In his grief, he wouldn't let any of us touch him or offer him medical help in any way. Until, an older doctor approached him and engulfed him in a huge hug, saying, "I'm so sorry. It must be devastating, and I completely understand that you may not want to stop what is happening to you so you can follow your wife, and I will respect whatever you decide."

I lost my partner of sixteen years about five years ago. And it was devastating.

He'd been sick for some time, and in and out of hospital for the last weeks of his life. In some ways, his death came as a relief. After weeks of being by his side in the hospital, and going home only to sleep and change clothes, I could finally rest. I felt as if I was sleepwalking as I dealt with the funeral home, his funeral, the endless paperwork of death, banks, and more.

None of it felt real. And the grief was there, like an endless numb emptiness.

As the weeks went by, friends stopped dropping in. My grown-up children went back to their lives and husbands. I went through the motions of living. Much of the time I really didn't want to live anymore. It just seemed too hard, too painful.

But my kids had already lost their stepfather, so I had to find a way to stay alive. The only way to do that was to work through the pain and grief I was feeling and find some way through to the other side.

I remember watching *Downton Abbey* at the time. One of the main characters lost her husband in a car racing accident. She proceeded to spend a whole year, clad in black, mourning. She wandered around like a lost, pale, beautiful ghost while her family and the staff catered to her, fed her and worried over her. She wasn't expected to lift a finger to do anything practical. Nobody expected her to function. She had space to grieve, cry and be miserable, whereas I had a few days off work and the funeral. After that, everyone pretty much expected me to get back to normal.

Except I couldn't.

I still can't.

I tried counselling, and it helped a bit. It helped me to understand that what I was going through was normal, but it didn't do anything to help with the pain. And I cried every day for two years. I cried on my way to work. I cried on my way home. I often found myself crying during the day, triggered by anything from a cute baby to a sad report on the news. I still cry.

One of the hardest things were my tears — are my tears. Our society, here in modern Australia, really doesn't cope with public displays of emotions. Deep grief makes us vulnerable to emotion. It makes you see and feel everything so much more intensely, and it doesn't go away. It's as if once your heart has been broken open, it stays open.

When emotions are meant to be kept tightly under wraps, this can be confronting to those around you. I had to find a place where I could let out all those feelings without making everyone uncomfortable. I started drawing and writing — and it helped.

Many years ago, when I was a depressed dark teenager, I didn't judge my feelings, as most teenagers don't. I dug around in them, wore black, painted skulls, and listened to soulful depressing music. And it helped!

I remembered a book I'd read at the time that made a lot of sense to me. The author insisted that life—all if it—is about learning and expressing patterns. And to shift a pattern, you have to live it fully.

When you are depressed and mourning, being surrounded by bright, cheerful things is painful. Our society often wants to distract people from their inner darkness by directing them to focus on pretty flowers, to wear bright colours, to do cheerful things — all in the name of getting over it. But our basic instinct is to do the exact opposite.

So, I went back to wearing black, drinking vodka, smoking cigarettes and listening to bad country music. It gave me a safe space for all of those awful feelings and thoughts at three in the morning when nobody else was around. I had a place where no-one could judge me for feeling broken and pathetic and lonely. And I wrote, and I drew.

My paintings and sculptures were created along the way. I never set out to make art. Scribbling random patterns, playing with clay, and putting colour on paper was merely a way of expressing what I was experiencing and feeling. It was a way to get what was inside my head and heart out, so I didn't explode.

This journal is the kind of workbook I would have needed when I was going through the worst of my grief. Something that showed me the importance of expressing my pain, fear and sorrow, and helped me to do so, would have helped me so much. And I'm hoping this workbook can be a kind of helping hand, reaching out to help as you struggle to find your way through the labyrinth.

The idea came to me while I was looking through the photos of what I have created in these last few years. One series of sculptures and pictures came about after a painful breakup last year. I locked myself in the ceramic studio for a month, listening to sad love songs, crying, and making fragile battered and broken hearts — one for each relationship I have mourned. They were my lost loves, my dead partner, past boyfriends, my father, all the people who had broken my heart at one time or another. It was so painful — and so therapeutic.

I got to thinking about designing a journal for others to use to help them heal. It would be a space for all those feelings that we can't share with anyone else when we are too vulnerable, too sensitive, and let's face it, when no-one else wants to hear about them anymore. Eventually, even your best friends can tire of hearing about your lost love. Yet the pain remains … unless you find the space to let it out.

This is true for every heartbreak, be it through death, illness, or a breakup. So this journal is my gift to you. It is your place, where I'm going to encourage you to embrace, explore and let out all those thoughts and feelings that those around you may be telling you to get over. I don't think you can get over pain, grief and loss. The only way out is through.

Here, you can acknowledge and truly feel that awful pain. Cry with it, sob with it, dance with it, for however long it takes … until it is done.

CHAPTER TWO

How to use this journal

I've organised this book into sections, which contain questions for you to answer. The questions are there to get you started. The first time you read them, I suggest you answer each one quickly without thinking about it. You may well find that you go away and come up with a completely different answer — and that's fine! You can come back and write more!

You may also find that some of the questions make you angry or seem completely irrelevant. That's a valid response and just as useful as any other. Write that! See where it leads.

> "What a stupid *bleeping* question! Why the *bleep* should I answer that! How dare you ask! As if I'd ever tell anyone that ... (Actually, I did tell someone that once and they reacted really badly.)"

Do you see where this is going? You never know what you'll discover when you start to let things flow.

I also encourage you to swear, scribble, cross things out, write over the top of the printed pictures, add pictures of your own, stick in photographs or images from magazines. This journal is your safe space where you are allowed to be angry, scared, messy. And, you never have to show it to anyone. This is a workbook and journal, not memoirs to pass down to your grandchildren. You can write the sanitised version later if you want to. But, this is your messy recovery space.

RANDOM FAST SCRIBBLING:

One of the most useful writing techniques I know is from the book, *The Artist's Way* by Julia Cameron. The idea is that you simply start writing whatever random words come into your head. You write fast without stopping to think, filling at least two pages, and you don't go back and re-read what you've written. The technique is designed to allow your subconscious to come through your writing without your conscious mind getting in the way.

I use this technique a lot. As I write seemingly random stuff, I find that a pattern becomes clear in amongst it all. I might find myself repeating a word over and over, and then suddenly, I get the story around it. I've filled a lot of pages with swear words, or, "It hurts!!!" It can be incredibly soothing just to let it out!

And it is necessary. What you leave bottled up inside will eat away at you. The whole point of this journal is to open up and let it all spill out.

TALKING TO THE DEAD

It helps to talk to those we've lost. It's heartbreaking and at times infuriating that they don't talk back, so the conversation gets frustratingly one-sided. However, saying the things you need to say helps so much. Whether you think you are speaking to their spirit or a memory of them in your head really doesn't matter.

I still talk to my dead ex. In the beginning, I spoke to him all the time, and it was hard not being able to hear his deep gravelly voice answer me anymore. I got impressions of him, and I was never sure if they were real or what I imagined he would say if he was there next to me. Either way, it was conversation I needed to have. I would have gone crazy without it.

Okay, there's a decent chance talking to him proves that I was or am pretty crazy in many people eyes. But, I am in good company. Most of the people I have met who have lost a loved one speak to them. Ocker truck drivers have told me about seeing their mother's ghost and known down-to-earth cleaners who get visits from their dead husbands.

If you've lost someone you loved deeply, you need to be able to tell them everything you are feeling. You may want to dedicate this whole journal to writing to them.

QUESTIONS

As well as questions to help get you thinking and writing, there are also check-in questions about things we tend to forget when we are grieving. You can answer all the questions or none of them. They are mere suggestions to get you started. You may find that you start writing one thing and that it triggers an entirely different train of thought. That's okay — follow that rabbit hole, wherever it leads!

This journal isn't chronological, it's a place of discovery. When you are writing about feelings, you are delving around in the murky, convoluted weirdness of your subconscious. It is supposed to be messy.

You may find that you can't face some of the questions. Just go on to the next chapter — it's okay. You can return in a week, a month, five years ... whenever you're ready is the right time. And now is the right time, to make a start.

the Sun loved the flower
sooo much that it
shared its Warmth...
and the flower flourished...

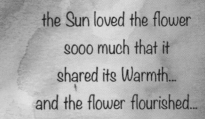

and as it grew, it's Joy
fed the Sun's Happiness
and in turn it grew &
glowed even brighter
Love can grow Abundance....
and another's Happiness
can feed and grow
and share Joy......

and this is how
it should be.

CHAPTER THREE

Right here, right now

——— CHECKING IN ———

Where are you?

Do you like it there?

How did you sleep last night?

Did you get dressed and have a shower?

Have you eaten today?

Where to begin? Right here and now. Take a breath and start with where you are. Feel whatever you are feeling and start writing. Random words are fine. Sentences that aren't connected are fine. Things that don't make sense or seem irrational are totally fine.

And a few prompts to get you started. In the beginning, it can be hard to do any of these things. The pain we feel when we have lost someone is so overwhelming that there is little or no room for anything else. The immensity of that great hole where someone used to be connected to your heart is so big that you can struggle to focus on any of the mundane day-to-day stuff.

Yet to survive, you have to pay attention to the ordinary day-to-day stuff. It can sometimes feel as if you are betraying the person you have lost by doing these things, or by just being alive when they are not. Or, that you are betraying the connection itself.

Truly, we might need somebody to take over for a while. But we don't always have someone who can do that for us. And often, we can quickly end up in the situation where there is no-one around who has the time, the patience, or the understanding of what we are going through, to listen to what we are feeling.

These basic check-in questions will be at the beginning of every chapter, because sometimes, the simplest things are the most important.

Close your eyes and feel within your body. Where do you hurt? Your heart? Your belly? Tell your journal about the pain. Our bodies always know. And sometimes, it is easier to listen to our bodies than our overactive confused minds.

This can be such a hard question to answer, especially in the early days of losing someone dear. I know I didn't want anything. For a long time, I felt as if I was in limbo, and everything was all too hard to even think about. Simple things like getting out of bed or making a cup of coffee took more energy and more presence of mind than I had.

Knowing what you need can be especially difficult if you have been looking after someone else for a long time. Life can revolve completely around the needs of the person you are caring for, so considering your needs and caring for yourself is something you must re-learn. This is why you will find the same basic questions repeated through this book. They are here to remind you to check in on what you need, and to look after yourself.

Sometimes the answers you come up with might seem weird, or even a bit crazy. It's okay — you can be crazy here. You don't need to hide anything. This journal is one place you can express all the weird, crazy out-there thoughts, feelings, dreams, insecurities, and whatever else, in complete safety. Remember, you never need to show this to anyone. Unless you choose to, and then it is up to you who you trust enough to share with.

It's your space.

CHAPTER FOUR

The small things

—— CHECKING IN ——

Where are you?

Do you like it there?

How did you sleep last night?

Did you get dressed and have a shower?

Have you eaten today?

Sometimes you need to bring your focus down to really small things. After my partner's funeral, I ran away to a friend who lived out in the bush. He lived in a large shack overlooking a beautiful valley. It was simple living, with two gas rings and a wood stove. To take a bath, you lit a fire under an outside cast iron bathtub. There was clear water from a spring up behind the house, and trees.

I developed a very close relationship with two of the trees outside the house — beautiful tall red cedars. I could see them from the bedroom window, where I spent a lot of my time.

I watched their bark and leaves change with the seasons, from summer to winter and spring. I could feel the strength of their tall, straight trunks, and below the ground, roots that ran as deep as their branches reached upward. These trees sustained me in a way I couldn't put into words. I held on to them, lived through them ...

I photographed them and drew them ... clumsily. Not as works of art, but as a way of connecting. It was a way to put the magic I could see and feel in these trees into pictures.

A little glimpse of tree, from a little box. My whole world. Safe.

Each day, my friend and I would go into town. He'd drive, I'd sit in the passenger seat. He'd go down the road and play dominos with his mates. I sat in a cafe at the other end of town, and order coffee, and draw.

I drew one simple pattern in a box for the day. Then he'd pick me up, and we'd buy food for dinner and drive back up the mountain, home. Sometimes it helps to simplify things.

I bought myself a soy cappuccino every day. And bottles of vodka. Then there was the gin and tonic phase. I consciously took up smoking after the funeral, because I needed something to hold on to. Looking after one's health can seem completely meaningless when your hurting. And anything that helps to ease the pain is a good thing. Eat the damn chocolate, stuff your face full of chips while you cry. If it helps, it's okay. So don't judge yourself.

Are there any clothes you like wearing? You know, those comfortable ones, that are the right colour, the right shape and material.

Look around and tell me about something small.

Do you have a favourite pillow?

A place where you like to sit?

What can you see out the window?

Is there a food or drink that brings you comfort?

Do you have a favourite t-shirt?

Are you living in a comforting dressing gown? If so, what's right about it?

What happens when you try to hide beneath the arm of someone who's weaker than you? When you need them to be as strong

2nd July '16 Cronawa

the little planet free floating in the
wide wide universe. It's light shining
brightly, bravely, but unsure if it is alone
in the Universe, or when it will find
other life...

7/2016

CHAPTER FIVE

Who have you lost?

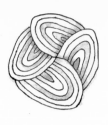

—— CHECKING IN ——

Where are you?

Do you like it there?

How did you sleep last night?

Did you get dressed and have a shower?

Have you eaten today?

This is a place where you can talk about the person/people you have lost. This can be hard to do, so if you need to, feel free to skip this chapter and come back to it later.

I couldn't comfortably talk about my man for years after he died — it was just too emotional. When I tried, I would invariably burst into tears halfway through. Which was particularly embarrassing if I was being asked about him by someone I didn't know very well.

But if you can …

What was their name?

Did they have a nickname? Or, different names amongst different people?

What was your relationship?

Where were they born?

What kind of person were they?

What kind of clothes did they like to wear?

What were their favourite songs?

What do you miss about them, most?

ever so beautifull
to Me....

David.. when are you how? You seem so much deeper in me.. smile I cu...

But I want to so so much interest in me.. I've felt so lost, I'm here sun when

Drew and David, and their imagined, I'm here dearly, but ever

any bravado that was you alive, as spirit, dearly, but ever

You stayed with me I loved you so when you well end all

my only sunshine, you make me happy, when skies are grey going

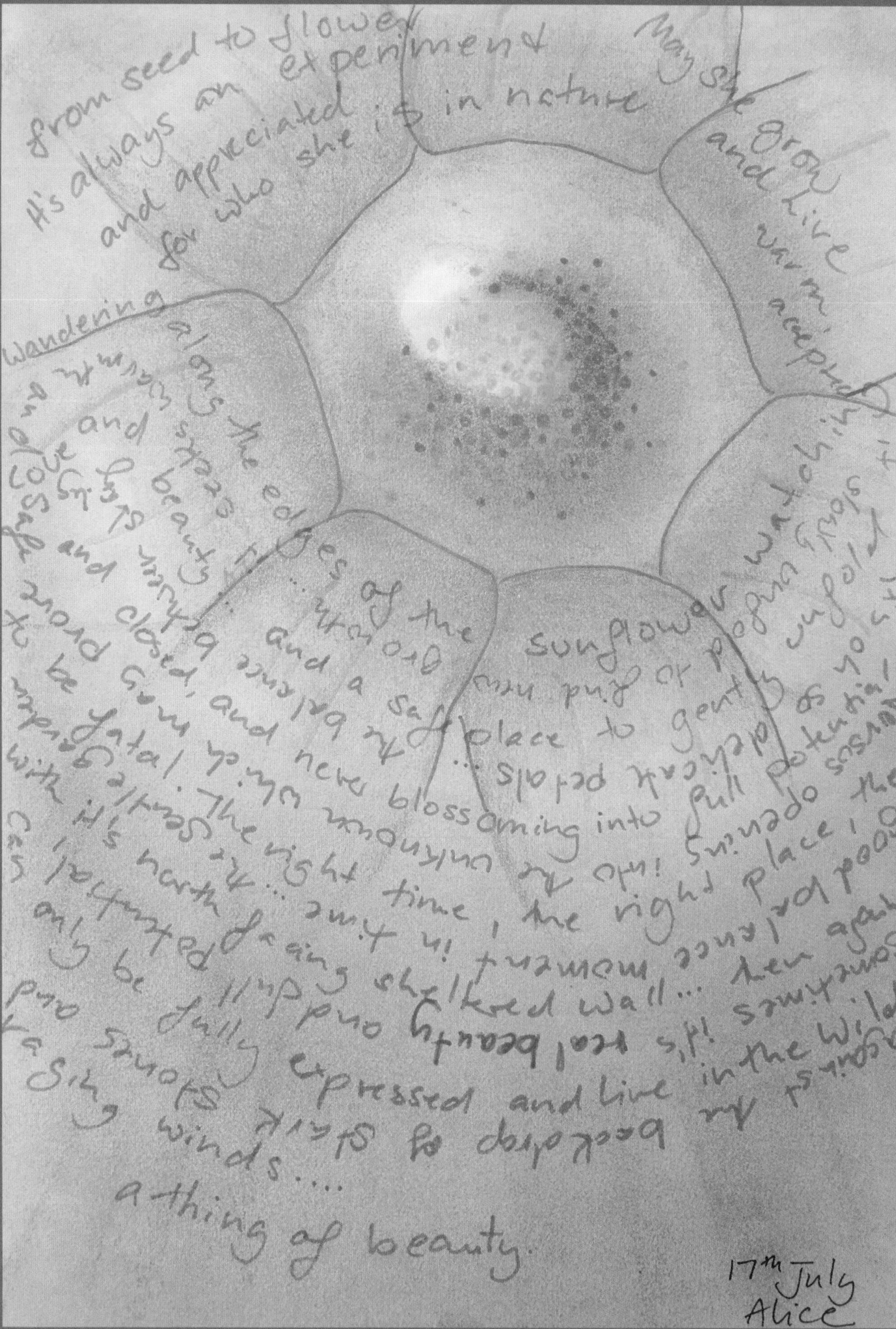

from seed to flower ... experiment

It's always an experiment
and appreciated
for who she is in nature

May she grow
and thrive
warm acceptance ...

Wandering along the edges of the
and beauty
love and closed, and never blossoming into full potential
safe ... to be fatal. The right time, the right place
with it's harsh ... being sheltered wall... then again

and a safe place to gently unfold
watching ...
sunflower ... and find new ground!

sometimes it's real beauty can
only be fully expressed and live in the wild
a backdrop of still moments and
a rising winds....

a thing of beauty.

17th July
Alice

my little world
8/3/17

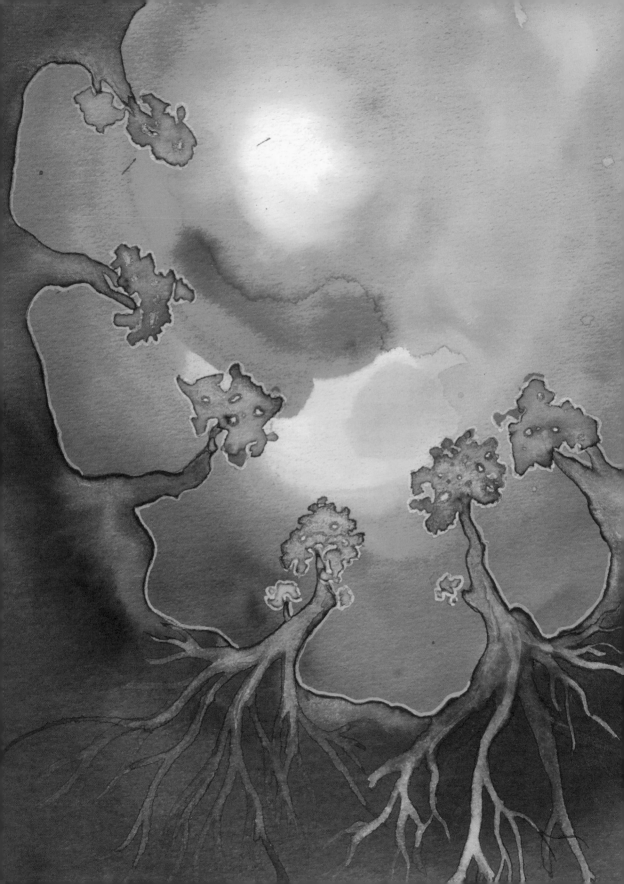

CHAPTER SIX

How did you lose them?

—— CHECKING IN ——

Where are you?

Do you like it there?

How did you sleep last night?

Did you get dressed and have a shower?

Have you eaten today?

We often need to find the words and tell this story many times over until the sharpness of the memory dulls a little. I needed to tell it again and again. I recently wrote down how my partner died. I was surprised at how many of the details I hadn't thought about for a while. And, at how much pain was still attached to the memory, six years later.

Many people who have been through traumatic events will relive them over and over. Sometimes the only way out of the recurring pain is to talk, to write, to go back there. Consciously revisiting the cause of our heartache can take some of the sting out of it, so that it stops hurting so unbearably.

The last weeks, the final moments, the unexpected shock, the horror, the what-ifs, the maybes, if you were or if you weren't there … It can be a nightmare that plays over and over in your head or a sad but beautiful memory of the last moments you held them in your arms before they slipped away peacefully. It is your memory, and it is important.

How did it happen?

Where you there?

Was anyone else?

What did you do then?

How do you feel about how they died?

What was your relationship?

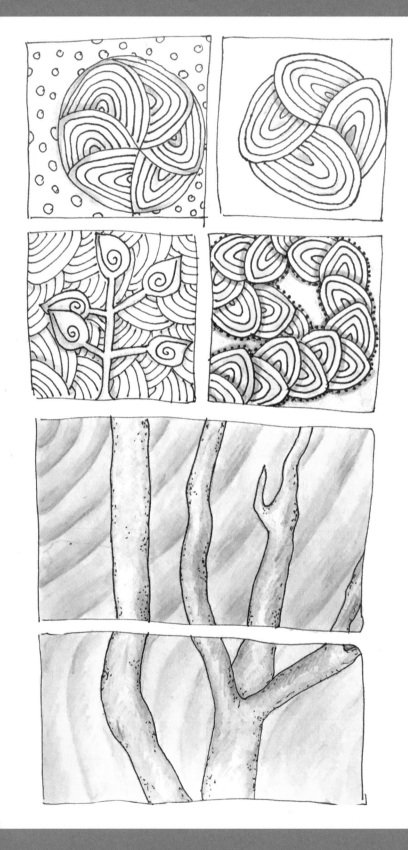

CHAPTER SEVEN

Best memories

—— CHECKING IN ——

Where are you?

Do you like it there?

How did you sleep last night?

Did you get dressed and have a shower?

Have you eaten today?

This is the bit people expect a grieving person to talk about. It's the things we stand up and say at funerals, the pretty nice stuff, the good memories. This is the socially allowable chapter, and a hugely important one.

If we didn't have oodles of good memories, the person would not be so precious to us and losing them wouldn't be so hard. And it's often the little things we miss most.

What is it that you miss?

What is one of the best times you can remember?

What did you love about them?

What did you learn from them?

What made them different from everybody else?

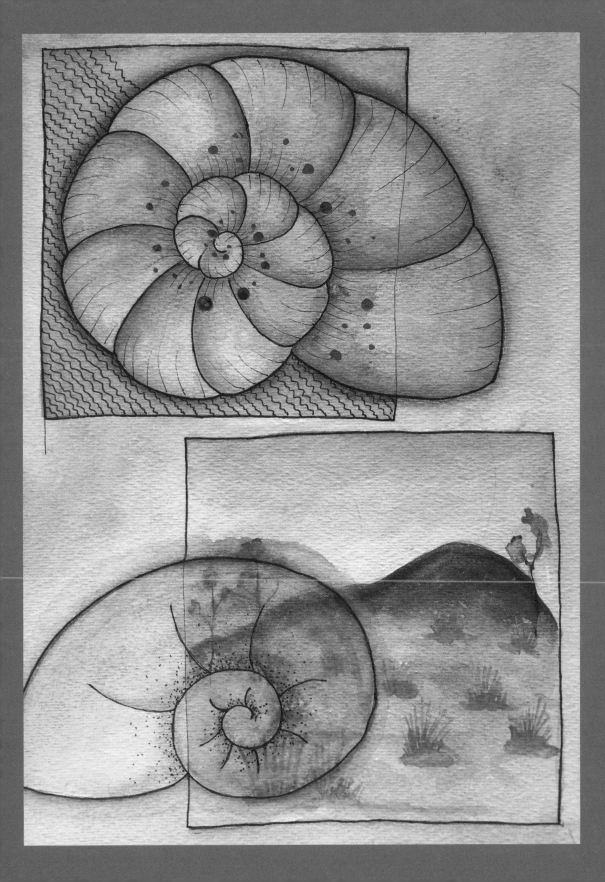

Opening the Abyss is beyond terrifying...
It lurks beneath, bubbling away at the
underneath the surface below... wanting to
explode out and take over the universe...
but it's also like a painful cyst that need to
be lanced... that way the pressure can be let
out... and energy is just energy... everything ca
be transformed...
And creation can commence anew.

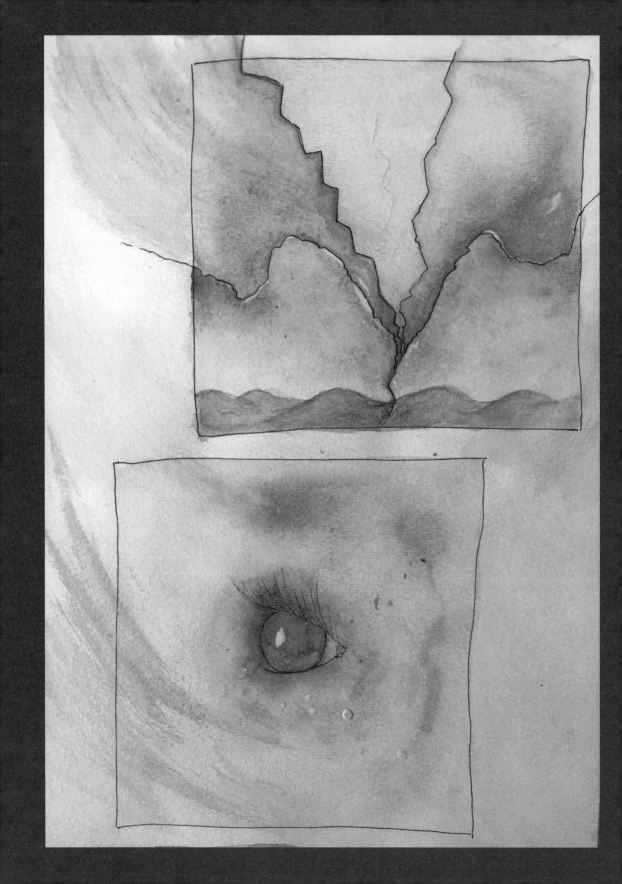

CHAPTER EIGHT

A place to be angry

—— CHECKING IN ——

Where are you?

Do you like it there?

How did you sleep last night?

Did you get dressed and have a shower?

Have you eaten today?

Everyone has their light and dark sides. Yet, when someone dies, we are expected to wash over their imperfections and only remember the best of them. This idea is unhelpful. They were real, whole people and we need to claim all the memories—the good, the bad and the ugly—to be able to work through our loss.

Not speaking ill of the dead is an unuseful sentiment that turns the person we've lost into some kind of plastic saint. It erases half their reality. And it blocks the grieving process.

Elisabeth Kübler-Ross outlined the stages of grief to include denial, anger, bargaining, depression and acceptance. Of these, anger can be the hardest because it's the one we block out. We can feel guilty for being angry. After all, if we truly loved someone and miss them, wouldn't we be sad or grateful to have known them at all? Instead, there is resentment, fury, and so many more layers of anger as well.

We can be vexed over bad memories, outraged about them dying, resentful about being left behind to deal with all the shit of day-to-day living, and angry about hurting so bloody much. I finally tapped into a little of my anger a few years after my partner died. It was three in the morning, the usual time for my deepest, darkest soul confrontations, and instead of wallowing in pain and self-pity, I got mad. Once the anger surfaced, I was shocked at how much was ready to come out. I ended up standing out on the road in the dark screaming at him.

I was angry at him for leaving me, mad at him for all the small (and big) shitty things he'd done when we were together, and screamingly furious at him for hanging around with an angelic ghost smile telling me everything was going to be okay. Because it wasn't, and I told him so.

"It's not okay, and I'm not okay! And I hurt and I don't know how to cope, or make it stop! And you SUCK!!!!"

And then I broke down and cried again.

Goddess knows what the neighbours thought of this madwoman out on the street screaming at 3am. But I felt ... better. After that, I started to write about the shitty things in our history — the bad stuff, the annoying stuff, the things I hated about him when he was alive, and it helped to put things in perspective.

I began to see him as a real person again, not just the idealised romantic love of my life who could never be replaced. It helped me to cherish him and the time we'd had together. It also helped me to begin to let him go.

So go for it!

You're allowed to be angry!

Resentful!

Ungrateful!

Completely unreasonable!

After all, who's around to judge you for it? Start writing and see what comes up. And, if you need to take a break to go and scream or throw rocks, know you're in good company. :)

What are some of the worst memories you have of your loved one?

What little things about them really pissed you off?

Which things didn't you love?

What kind of annoying habits and quirks did they have?

What are you angry about right now?

What do you resent?

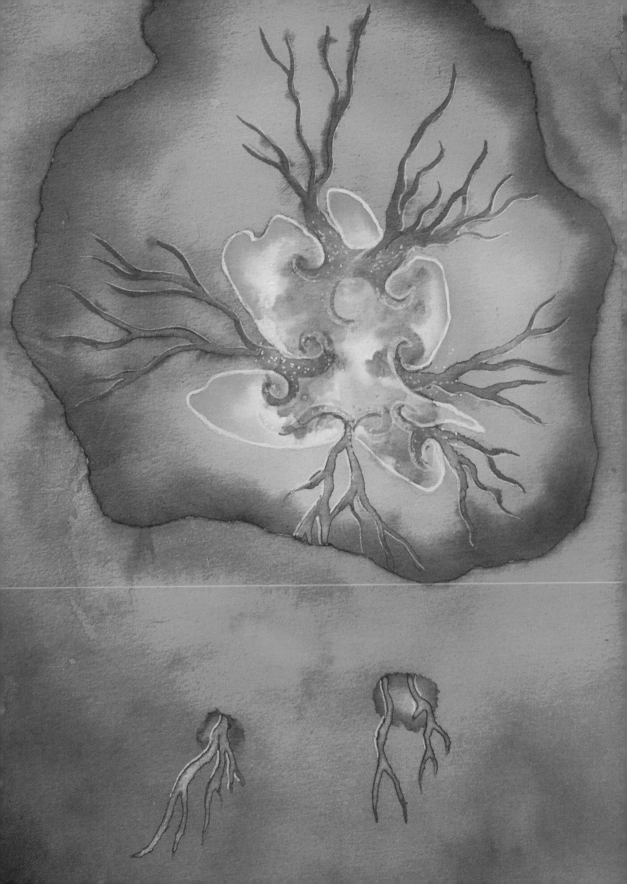

CHAPTER NINE

Regrets

—— CHECKING IN ——

Where are you?

Do you like it there?

How did you sleep last night?

Did you get dressed and have a shower?

Have you eaten today?

What do you wish you had done and said — or not done and said? Here is a place to wallow and dig out your regrets, the things you think you did wrong, and all the opportunities you missed. When you allow yourself full reign to go into the deep parts of these regrets, you may come to realise that things did work out the way they were supposed to. Sometimes, of course, that's just not so. And there are real things you woulda-shoulda-coulda done. And if that's the case, it's time to face it.

So, voice just how badly you stuffed up. You can rant, cry, beat yourself up over it, and then, move on. You can't go back and fix the past, but you can face it, own it, learn from it, and then do better.

Many people have started foundations and charity organisations after the death of a loved one. This can be as a tribute or because they felt the need to do something to make up for what they perceived as having missed or not done for the person they loved and lost. Maybe this reveals some of the good that can be found in loss and grief. It can be an impetus for change and creating new things.

Is there anything you regret not having done or not having said to your loved one?

Is there anything you wish you had done or said?

What stopped you?

Is there anything you wish you hadn't done or said?

Why did you do it? (Or say it?)

What can you do now or in future that is different?

new growth...

...Lonliness...

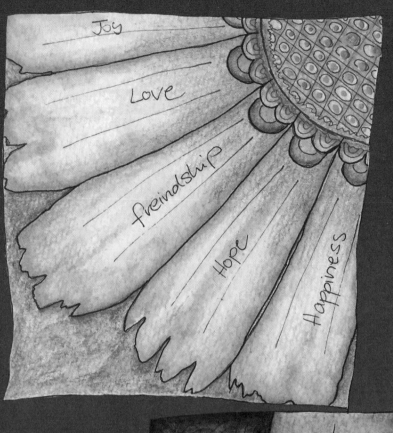

CHAPTER TEN

Dreams

---- CHECKING IN ----

Where are you?

Do you like it there?

How did you sleep last night?

Did you get dressed and have a shower?

Have you eaten today?

In the year after I lost my partner, there was a period where I would wake at three in the morning, panicking from horrendous nightmares. Every. Single. Night. For months.

A friend of mine who lost his baby son to cot death forty-eight hours after he was born, relived the same dream of desperately giving mouth-to-mouth to his newborn boy, over and over. And not just for months, for years.

My partner sometimes appears in my dreams, and it feels like he's visiting — just popping in to see how I'm doing. Nowadays, I usually wake up happy from these dreams. But sometimes still, it is gut-wrenching, because I wake up and he's not here.

Our dreams are our subconscious speaking to us. I also believe they are a place where those we have lost can sometimes wander in for real. It can be both beautiful and painful to wake up having been with someone you've lost — like losing them all over again.

Maybe that's why depression makes us want to sleep all the time? So we can wander around in the other world, because this one is just too hard to bear. Sleep is the place where our subconscious comes through, where our hidden fears, longings and needs come to the surface so that we can heal.

How often do you dream?

What do you dream?

How does that make you feel?

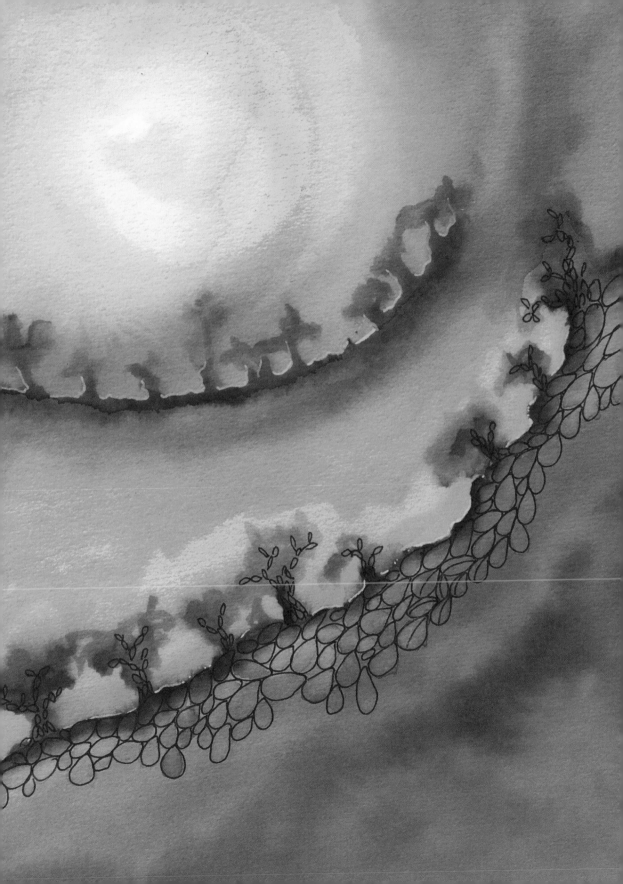

CHAPTER ELEVEN

Letting go

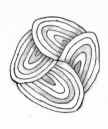

—— CHECKING IN ——

Where are you?

Do you like it there?

How did you sleep last night?

Did you get dressed and have a shower?

Have you eaten today?

Part of the grieving process is coming to a place where you can let go of the one you love. A first step is that awful task of dealing with their belongings.

After the funeral, my kids and I were left with all of my partner's stuff — his collections of personal things, clothes, tools, everything. None of us could do anything with them. Every time I went into his toolshed to start sorting things, I burst into tears.

I got to a point where I felt his spirit start nagging me about it. It was as though he was urging me on, telling me I needed to let him go and focus on those who were still physically here on this side ... where I was. But I couldn't.

It was too scary. Letting go made me feel much too alone.

In time, I did start to reconnect to those around me here. As more time went by, my memories of him began to fade — and that was scary, too. I felt, and still feel, guilty that I struggle to remember his face, his touch, his smell. However, life in the here and now became more real and vibrant than memory. And I could finally begin, little by little, to let go.

How do you feel about "letting go"?

Have you done anything to help this process?

Are you avoiding it?

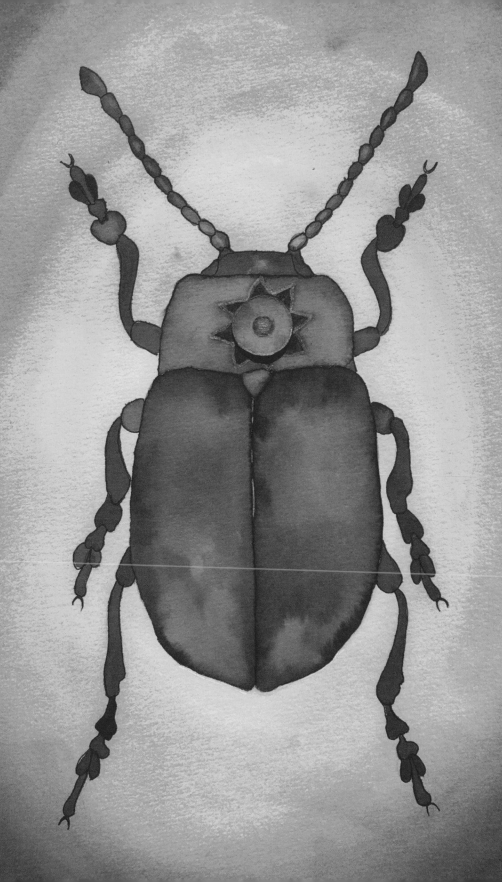

CHAPTER TWELVE

Where to now?

——— CHECKING IN ———

Where are you?

Do you like it there?

How did you sleep last night?

Did you get dressed and have a shower?

Have you eaten today?

Grief brings a weird kind of freedom with it. When you lose someone important to you, it brings the rest of your life into a different perspective. Nothing else seems that important anymore, not your job, your mortgage, or your holiday savings plan. Most importantly, it reminds you of your own mortality.

What has changed in you?

Does the world look different?

What is important to you now?

What are you doing?

What are you going to do next?

I started to write, "I'm not the same person I was before my partner died." But that's not really true. I am the same person, but my perspective has shifted. I am more open, more vulnerable, stronger, more confused, clearer.

Loss changes you. It shapes you, twists you and tears parts of you open that others seem able to keep under control. My emotions are far closer to the surface, now. I cry more easily during soppy movies, butterflies fill me with awe and small children glow in a way I wasn't aware of before.

I see people differently. Kindness in a person is now the most admirable thing to me, beyond any other quality. Loss also taught me humility. It revealed my frailty and the vulnerability in every human. We will all know grief and pain at some stage. Many people walk through life carrying the scars of huge loss, and it is usually invisible — but I see it now.

Grief has taught me to be more patient, more caring, and beyond all, to treasure love and connection in any way that I find it. I worry less about tomorrow and far less about money or career. Time itself has become precious. The connections and the love I have with others are now something sacred that I treasure above all else.

This journal isn't one I'd ever planned on writing. I was going to write an epic novel, a world-changing book on healing, become a famous artist. Instead, I penned a simple workbook, full of my pain and weakness and grief — and it helped. And now it's gone out into the world, and I hope it helps you, too.

If anything, know you aren't alone. Those of us who have gone through heartbreak know how much it hurts. It's okay to be broken. And, it's okay to hope, and to heal, and to love.

This is not the end. It's the beginning of something new, something different, something built from the heartache, pain, beauty, and everything you have experienced that has given you fresh depth and understanding.

There is a beautiful art form in Japanese culture called kintsukuroi, where pottery that has been broken is mended with pure gold, accentuating the break instead of seeking to cover it up. In this way, the history of the precious piece is honoured and celebrated, and its uniqueness makes it even more beautiful. My wish, my hope, is that writing in this journal may have helped you to begin to cherish your own broken heart in the same way!

Keep writing, keep crying, keep dancing and painting and singing. Keep moving through what you are feeling, rather than bottling it up, whatever it may be.

Much love and healing,

Ambrosia

" Everything will be all right in the end. If it's not all right, it is not yet the end. "

- THE BEST EXOTIC MARIGOLD HOTEL

About Ambrosia

Ambrosia Jones is an artist, healer and writer who works in watercolour, ceramics, felt, photography, scent, music and any other medium she puts her hands on. She specialises in what she calls Mystical Realism and her art is a reflection of how she sees and interacts with the world around her. Ambrosia uses vibrant colours to show the inherent magic and sacredness of Mother Earth and the energy that runs through her.

Much of Ambrosia's work is inspired by her extensive travels, living and working in outback Australia as a remote area nurse. She has worked with at-risk teenagers in outback schools, taught art therapy and run workshops and classes on energy healing and earth shamanism for three decades. She was the founder of the Blue Pentacle, a Pagan healing organisation focused on bridging the divide between modern medicine and alternative healing practices. She has also written articles and regular columns on traditional healing methods for different publications.

Ambrosia is the mother of three young women, grandmother to two boys, and honorary parental figure to seven 'extra-curricular' children, teens and young adults. She does her best to work anywhere she has access to art supplies – and as you won't find her travelling without watercolours, pencils and pens, that is everywhere, including on two-person planes on the way to remote area nursing jobs. Hand her unmoulded clay, a child, pigment or paper and she will produce something beautiful. Ambrosia has spent her life creating, bringing beauty to the world and comfort to all who need it as a mother, a nurse, and an artist.